AF338284

Zoey's Great
Adventures
Learns to Talk

Published in the United States by Yellow Daisy Publishing LLC
ISBN: 978-1-953556-01-1

Find more books like this, book an event, and get a free printable, visit our websites:
www.AJKikumoto.com
www.yellowdaisypub.com

Let's Get Social!

Instagram: @zoeysgreatadventures1

Facebook: Zoey's Great Adventures

Thank you to Charles Kikumoto, my husband; Joyce and Bruce Loveland, my mom and dad; Alycia Darby, my pageant coach; Crystal Swain-Bates, my book coach; Dana Ashford, my queen friend; Maria Miller, our Occupational Therapist; Apraxia Kids, and AHA, Inc. for their advice, guidance, and edits in creating this impactful book.

A portion of the proceeds of Zoey's Great Adventures will go to Apraxia Kids!! www.apraxia-kids.org

Dedicated to 4 of my kids, who endure the challenges of Apraxia of Speech. This book is based on their true-life experiences.

In loving memory of Rosebud (Rosy), our beloved family mini horse.

This book belongs to:

____

____

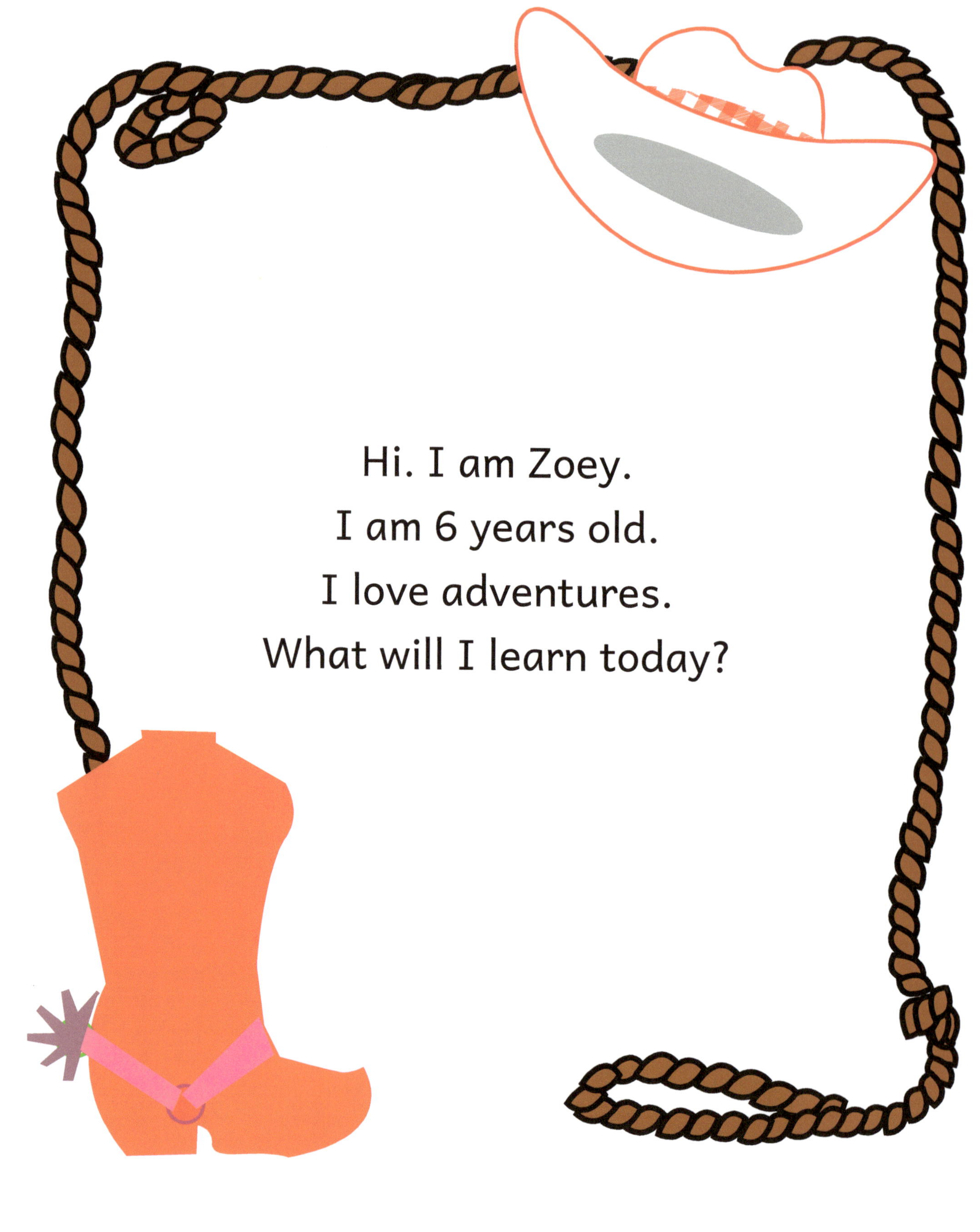
Hi. I am Zoey.
I am 6 years old.
I love adventures.
What will I learn today?

I have a horse.
His name is Crackerjack.
He is **brown** with white spots.
He has four white stockings.

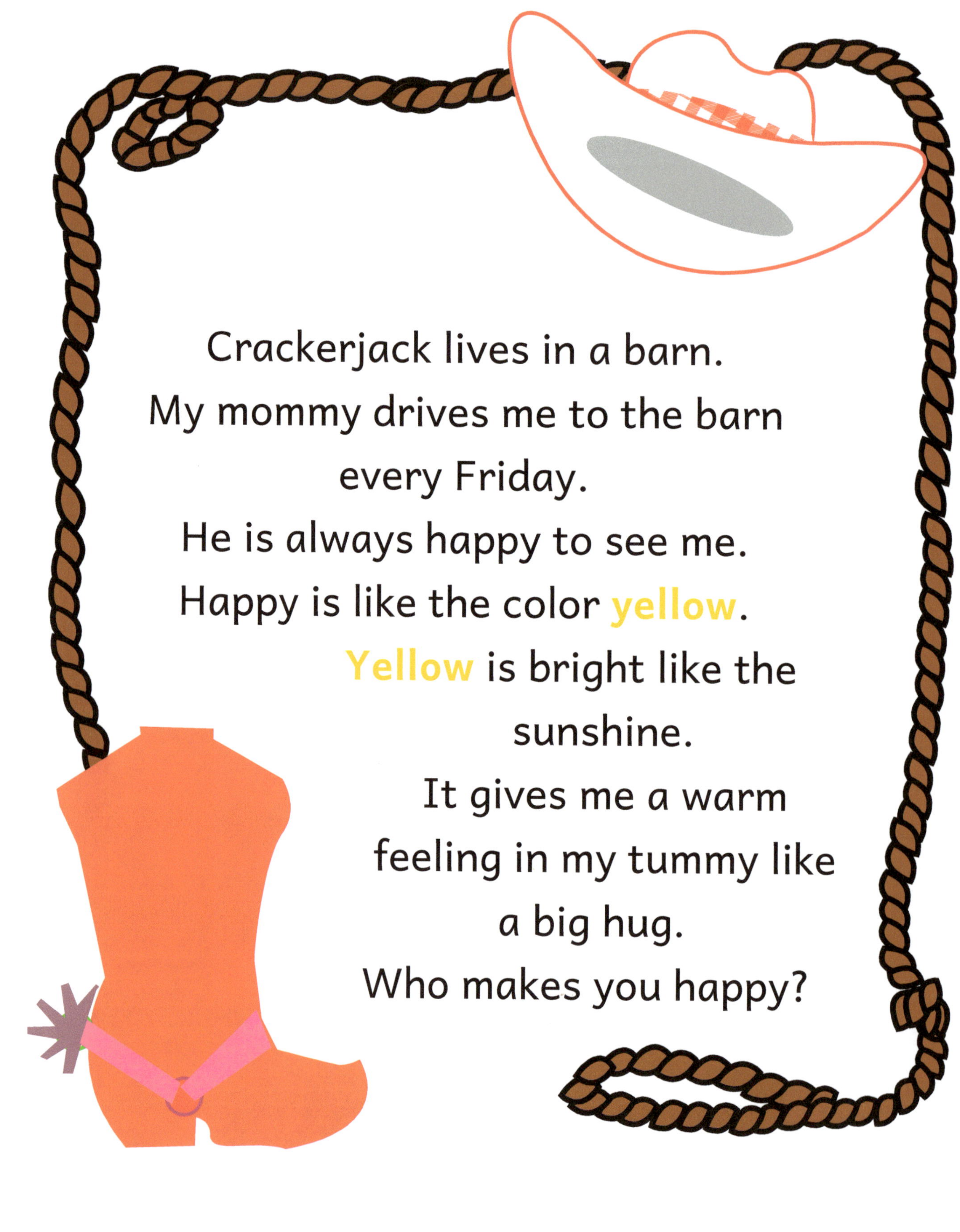
Crackerjack lives in a barn.
My mommy drives me to the barn
every Friday.
He is always happy to see me.
Happy is like the color yellow.
Yellow is bright like the
sunshine.
It gives me a warm
feeling in my tummy like
a big hug.
Who makes you happy?

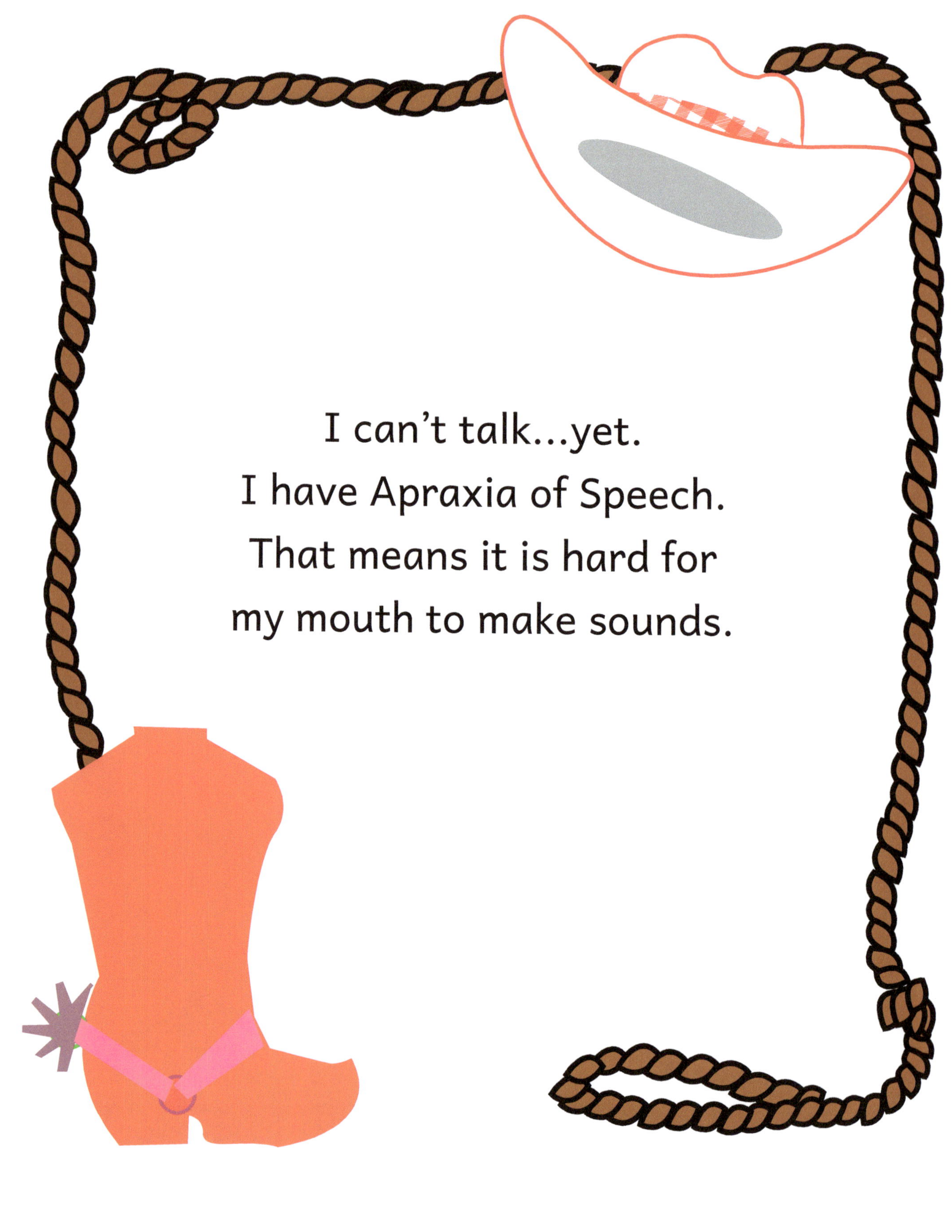

I can't talk…yet.
I have Apraxia of Speech.
That means it is hard for
my mouth to make sounds.

Some kids make fun of me because
I can't talk. It hurts my feelings.
It makes me feel sad.
Sad is like the color gray.
Gray feels like a
heavy cloud
is sticking to me.
It makes me want
to hide.

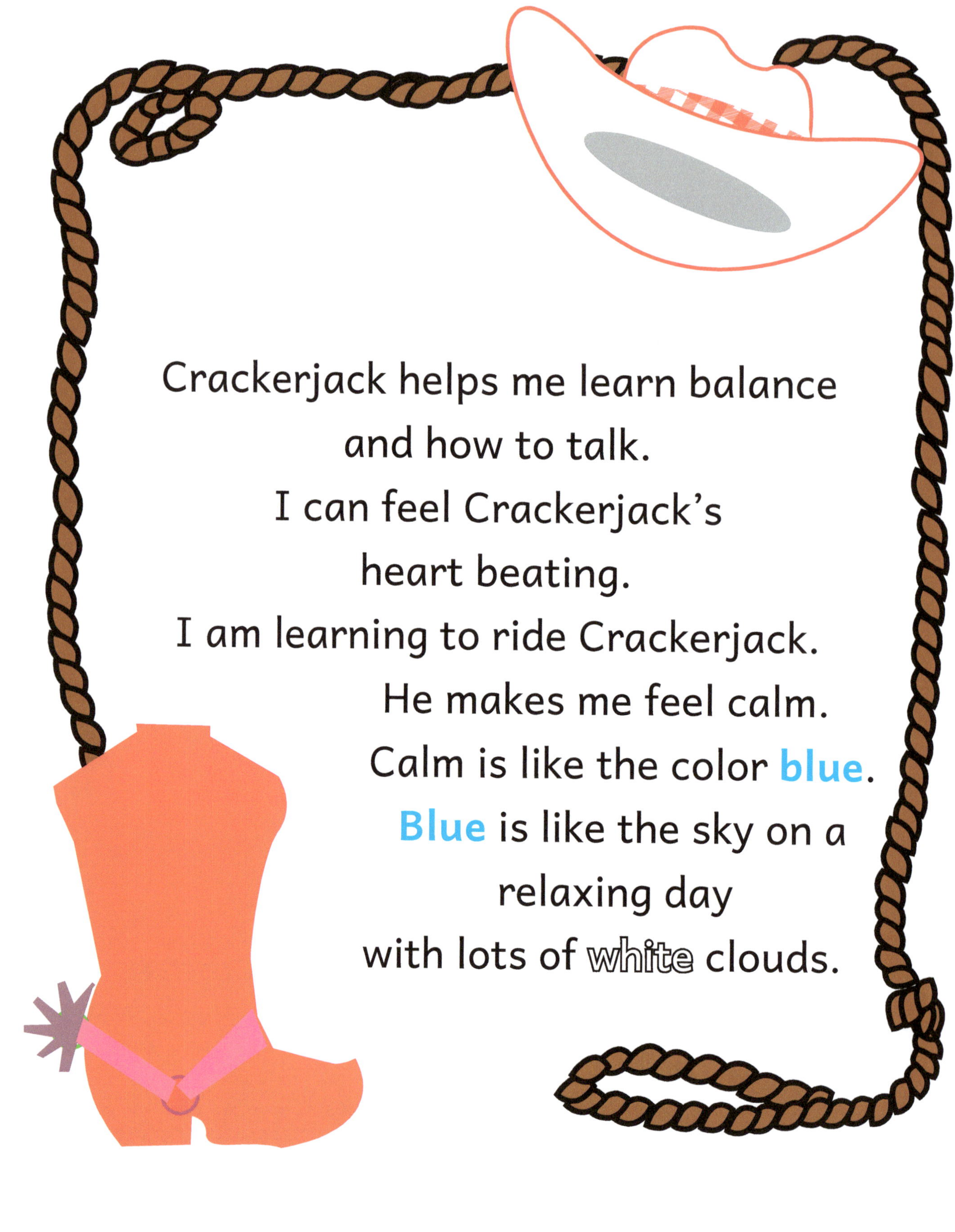

Crackerjack helps me learn balance
and how to talk.
I can feel Crackerjack's
heart beating.
I am learning to ride Crackerjack.
He makes me feel calm.
Calm is like the color **blue**.
Blue is like the sky on a
relaxing day
with lots of white clouds.

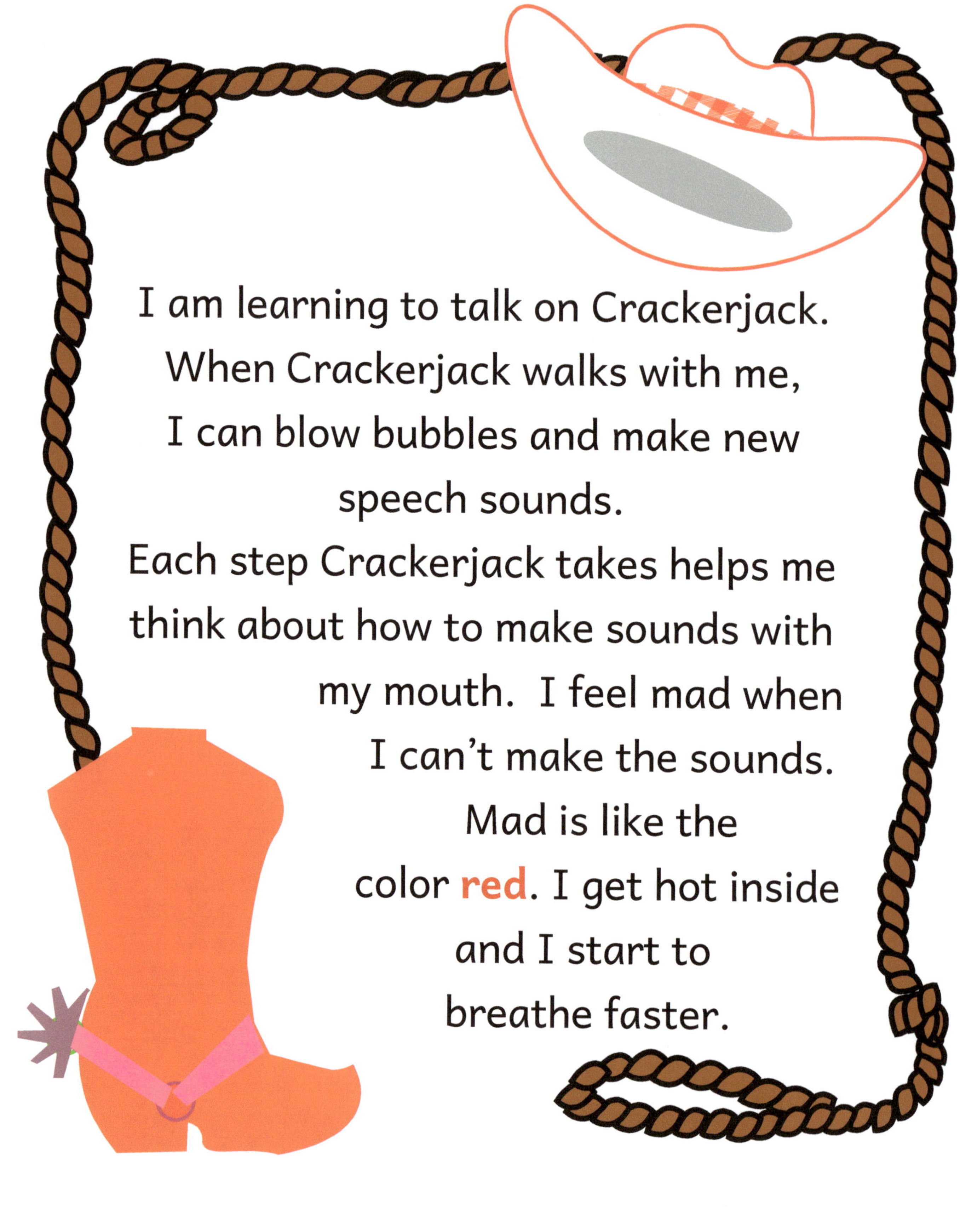

I am learning to talk on Crackerjack.
When Crackerjack walks with me,
I can blow bubbles and make new
speech sounds.
Each step Crackerjack takes helps me
think about how to make sounds with
my mouth. I feel mad when
I can't make the sounds.
Mad is like the
color red. I get hot inside
and I start to
breathe faster.

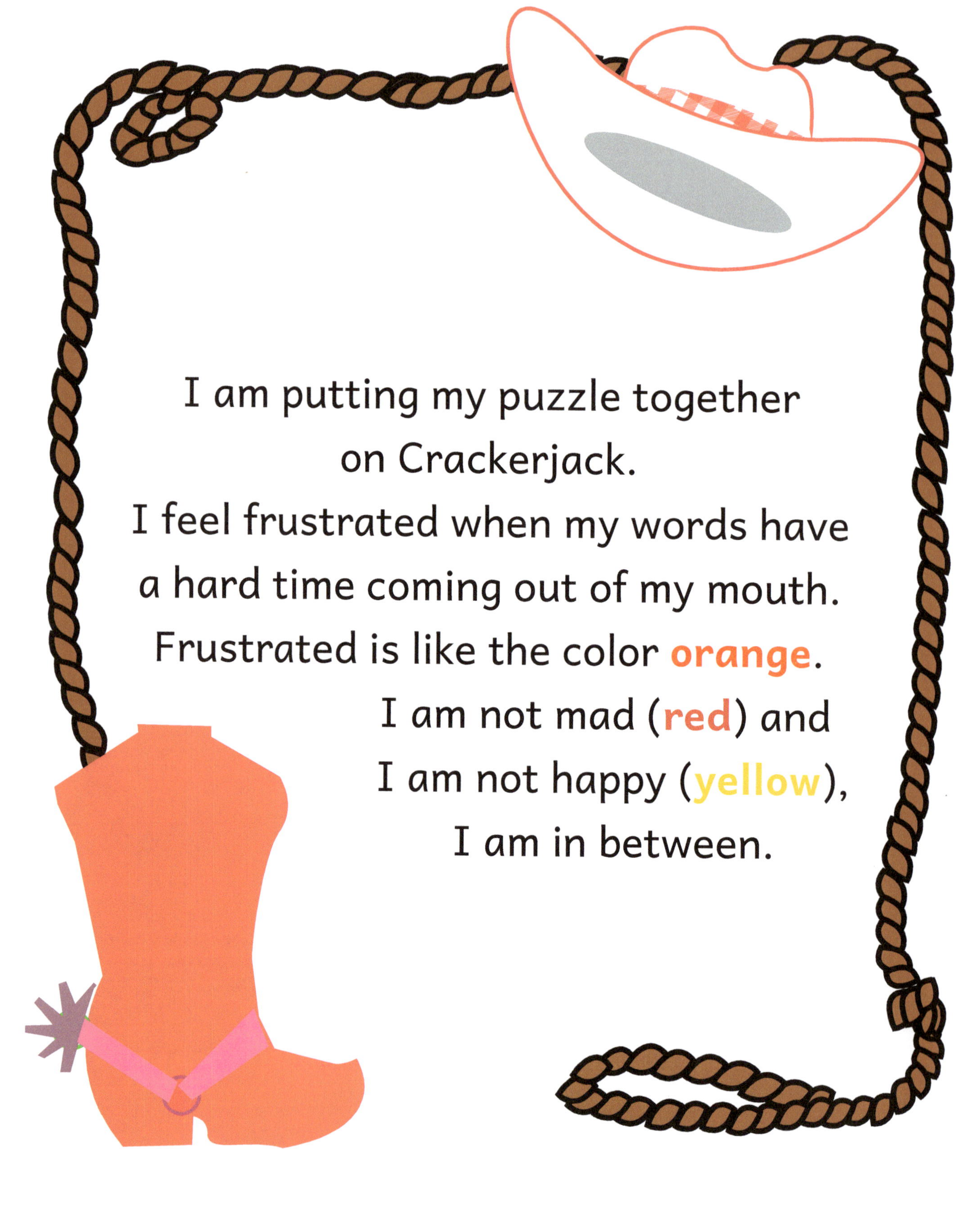

I am putting my puzzle together
on Crackerjack.
I feel frustrated when my words have
a hard time coming out of my mouth.
Frustrated is like the color orange.
I am not mad (red) and
I am not happy (yellow),
I am in between.

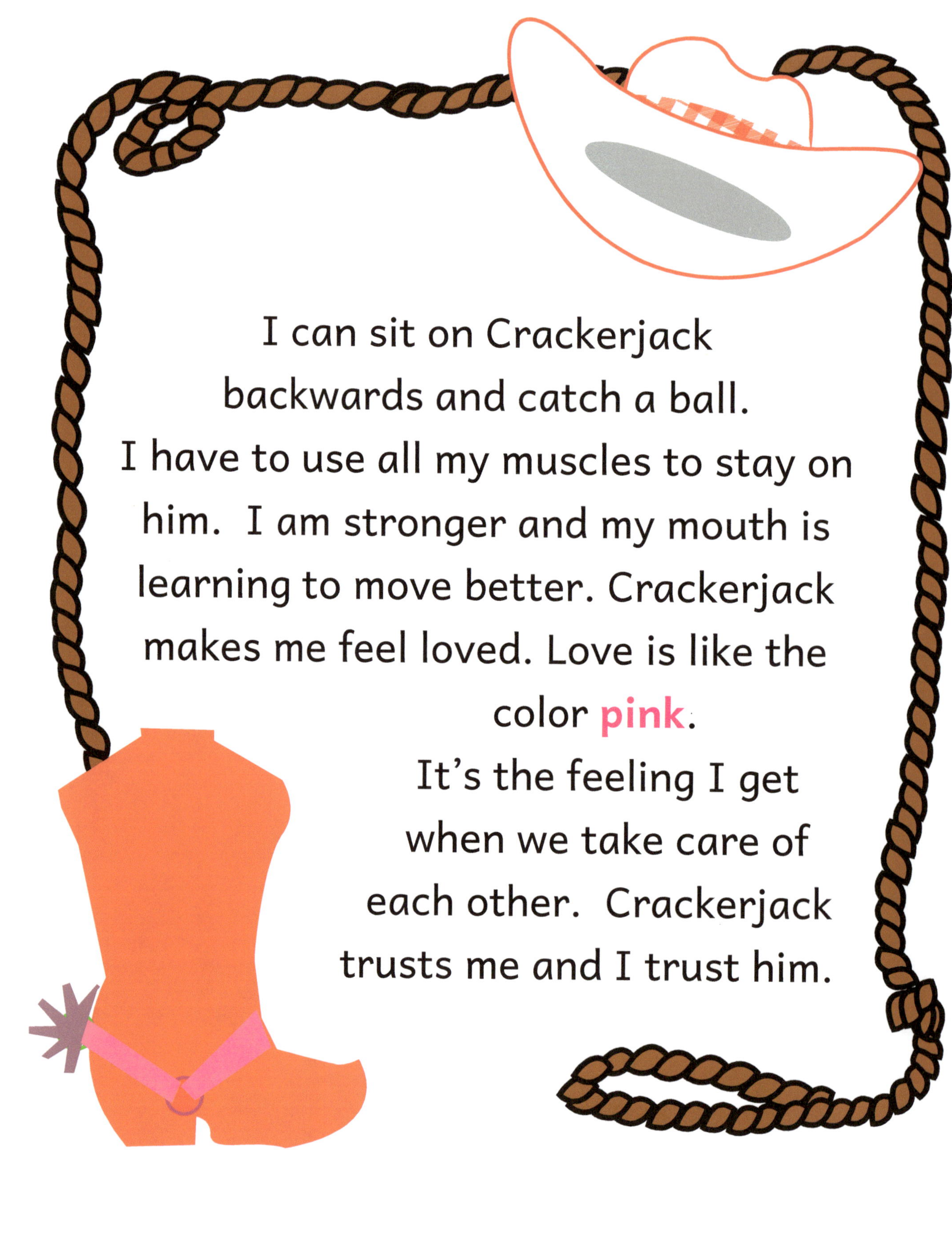

I can sit on Crackerjack
backwards and catch a ball.
I have to use all my muscles to stay on
him. I am stronger and my mouth is
learning to move better. Crackerjack
makes me feel loved. Love is like the
color pink.
It's the feeling I get
when we take care of
each other. Crackerjack
trusts me and I trust him.

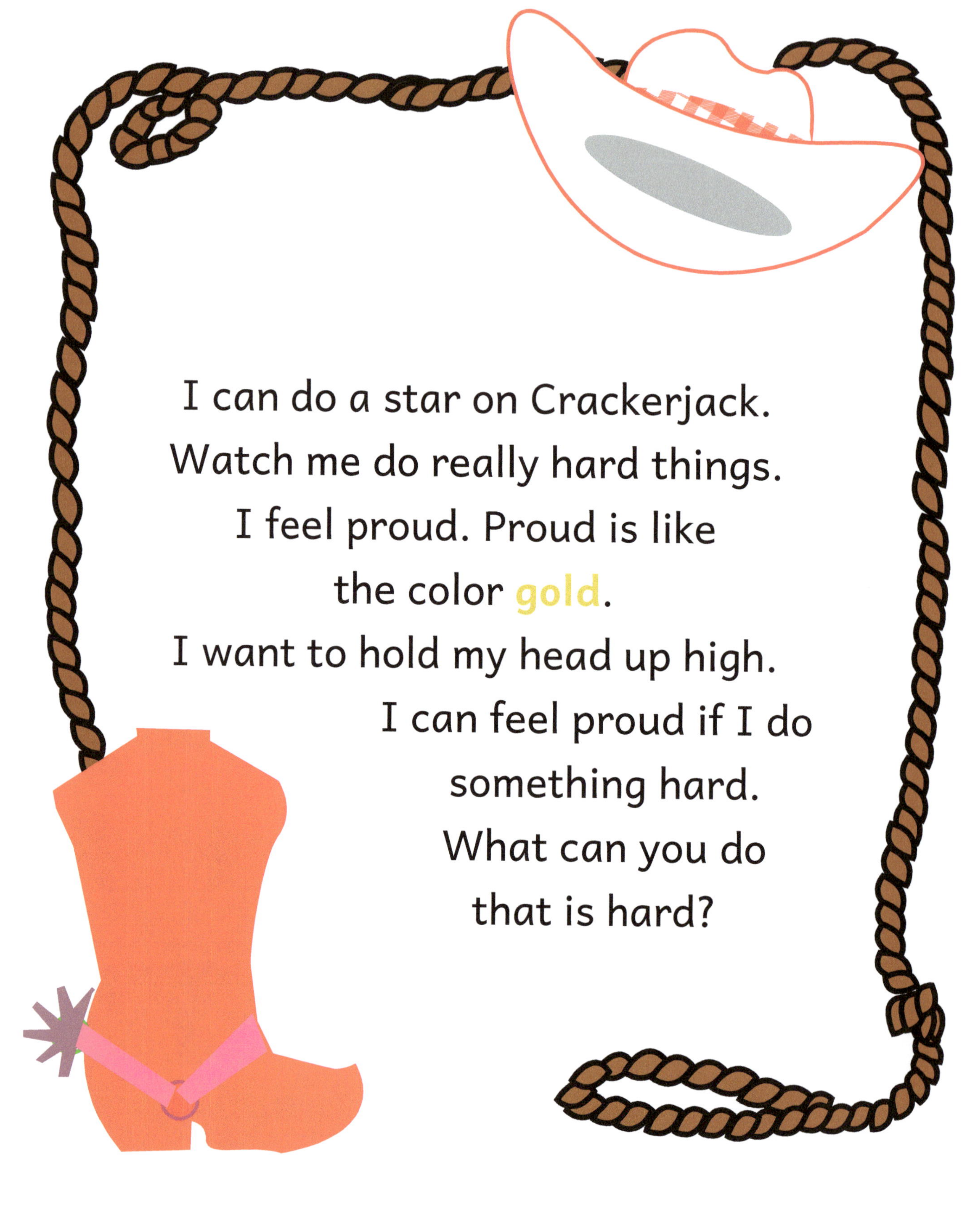

I can do a star on Crackerjack.
Watch me do really hard things.
I feel proud. Proud is like
the color gold.
I want to hold my head up high.
I can feel proud if I do
something hard.
What can you do
that is hard?

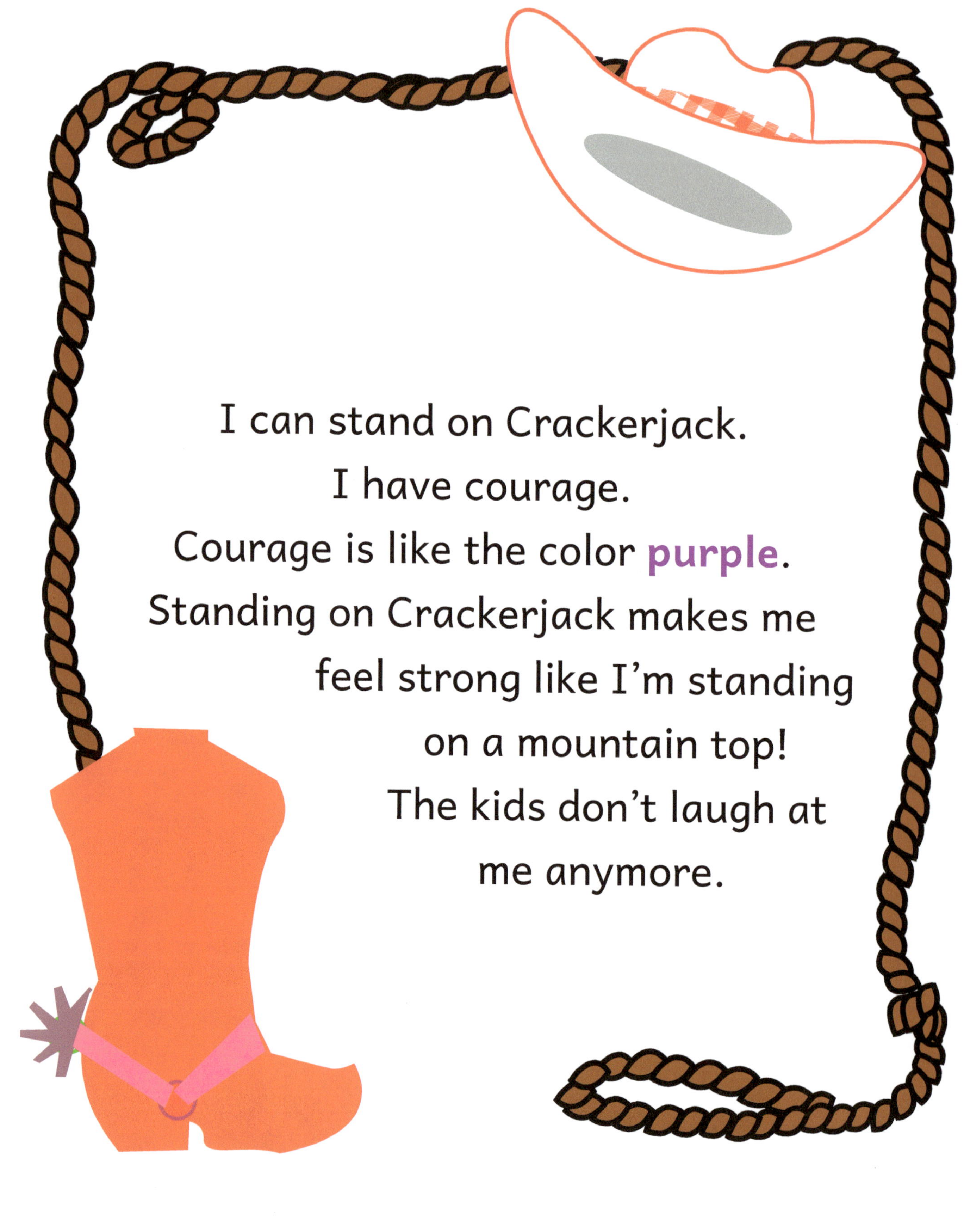

I can stand on Crackerjack.
I have courage.
Courage is like the color **purple**.
Standing on Crackerjack makes me
feel strong like I'm standing
on a mountain top!
The kids don't laugh at
me anymore.

Sometimes Crackerjack poops!
That is the color **brown**.
It makes me laugh.

My favorite thing to do on Crackerjack
is ride through the "car wash."
I love how the ribbons feel on my face.
They are the colors of the rainbow:
red, orange, yellow, green,
blue, and violet.
I learn to talk on
Crackerjack.
I tell him to "Walk On!"
That means
"Go" like the color green.

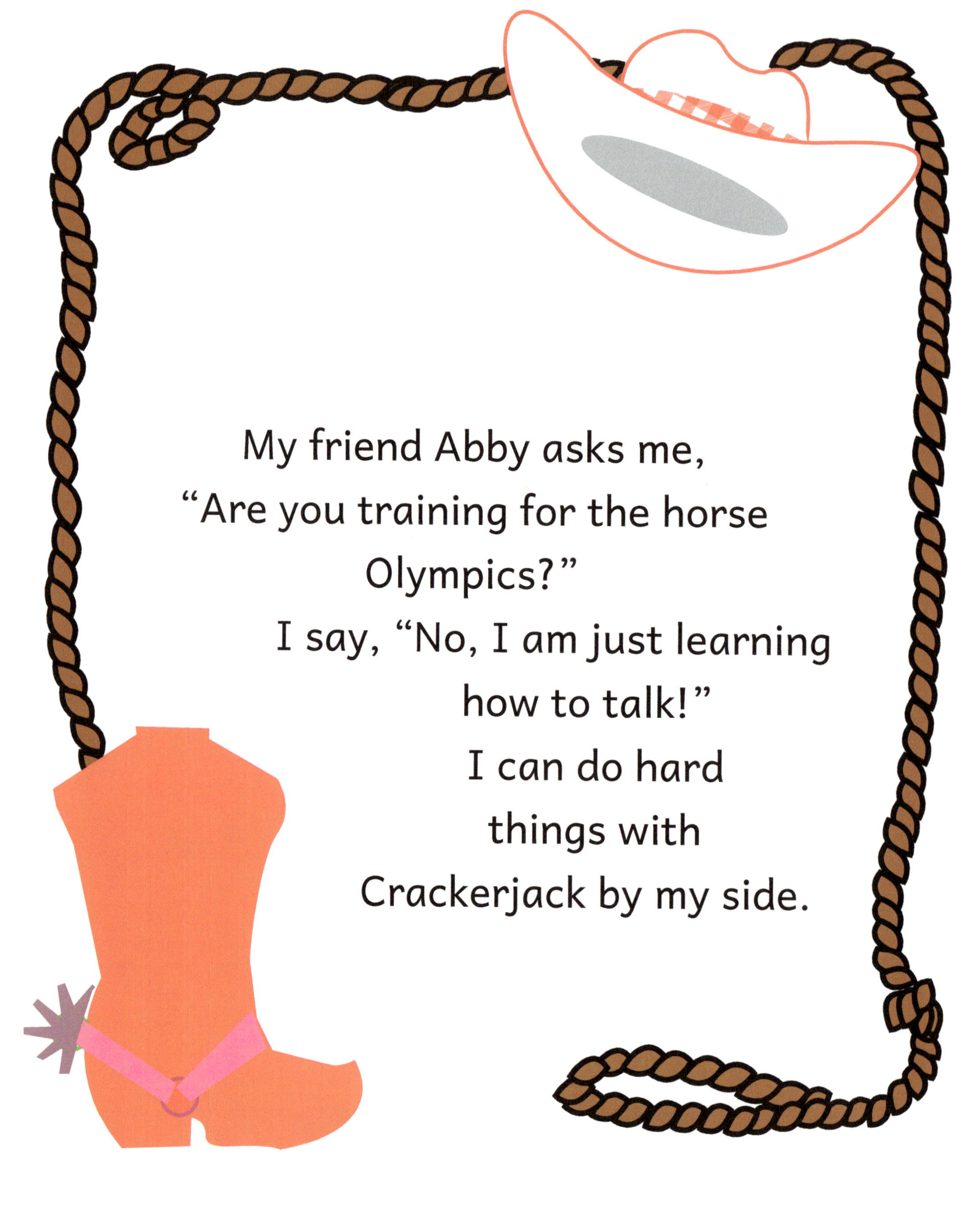

My friend Abby asks me,
"Are you training for the horse
Olympics?"
I say, "No, I am just learning
how to talk!"
I can do hard
things with
Crackerjack by my side.

WHAT IS CHILDHOOD APRAXIA OF SPEECH?

Childhood Apraxia of Speech (CAS) is a motor speech disorder that makes it difficult for children to speak. Children with the diagnosis of Apraxia of Speech generally have a good understanding of language and know what they want to say. However, they have difficulty learning or carrying out the complex sequenced movements that are necessary for intelligible speech. (www.apraxia-kids.org)

WHAT IS HIPPOTHERAPY?

The word hippotherapy comes from the ancient Greek word "hippos" meaning horse and "therapy" referring to treatment.

Hippotherapy is a treatment tool used in speech-language therapy as well as physical therapy and occupational therapy. Speech-language pathologists can use hippotherapy as a therapy tool to help develop the motor coordination for sequencing speech sounds among other things.

From the American Hippotherapy Association, Inc
https://www.americanhippotherapyassociation.org

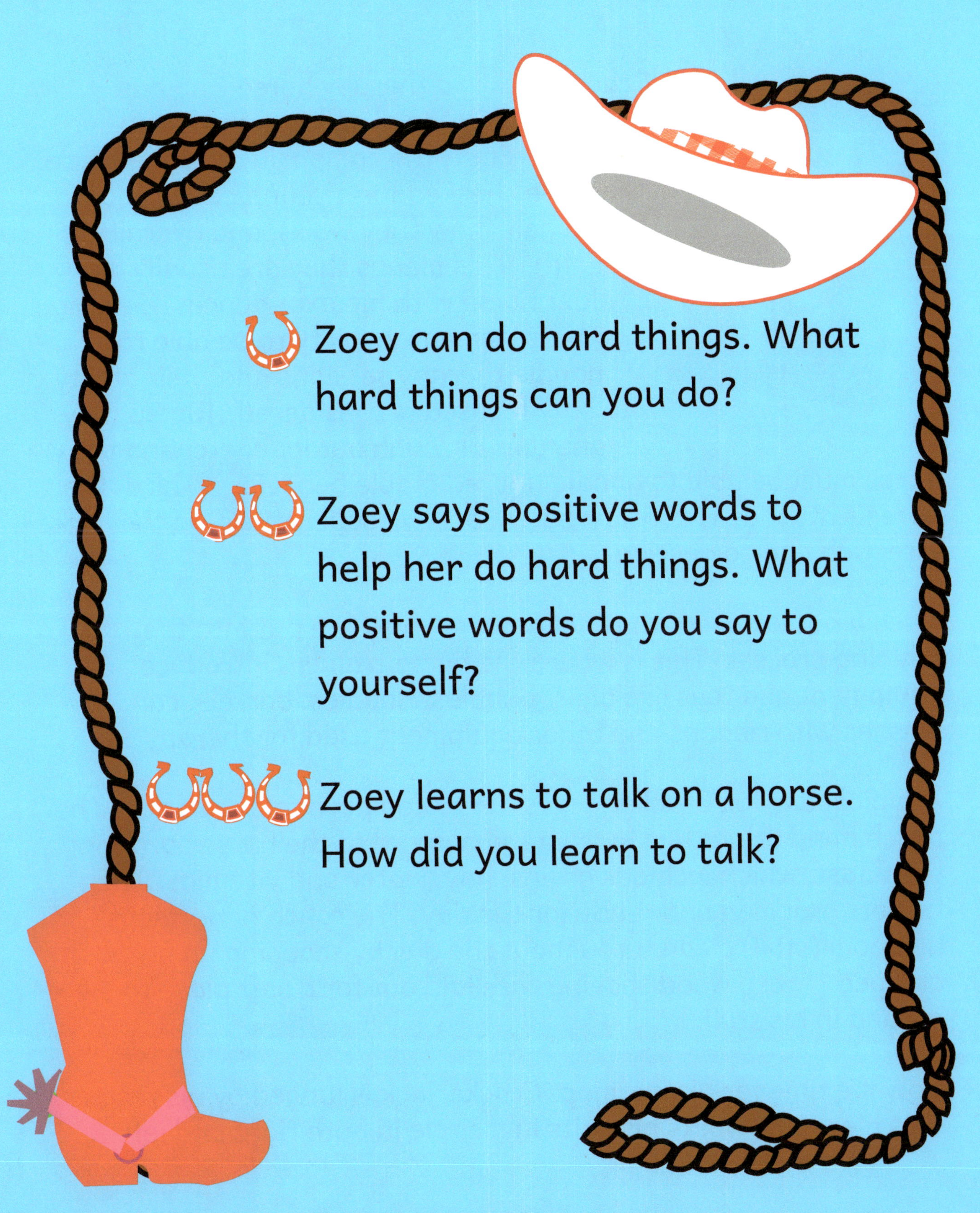

Zoey can do hard things. What hard things can you do?

Zoey says positive words to help her do hard things. What positive words do you say to yourself?

Zoey learns to talk on a horse. How did you learn to talk?

Meet the Horse

Crackerjack is a therapy horse who has been through a trial process and extensive training. First, the composition of the horse must be checked for a sound body, smooth, even gait (how they walk), and overall health. This means they are usually an older horse with life experiences. Second, a horse's mental ability to be able to handle therapy sessions and their ability to stay focused is considered. Riders may have tantrums or laugh out loud, etc, and the horse must be able to handle unpredictable behaviors. Third, the horse's attitude is considered. Are they cooperative? Do they take direction and correction?

Once a horse passes the trial process, they are put into the training process. This is where the horse trainers introduce equipment and toys like balls, bubbles, noodles, barrels, car washes with ribbons and other equipment used for therapy.

A typical day for Crackerjack is fun to compare to Zoey's day. The ranch hand brings him in from the pasture to the horse barn for breakfast, which includes grains, hay, water and vitamins. Then he gets groomed and ready for the day. The ranch hand keeps his room (stall) clean throughout the day by scooping up his poop and pee. Fresh wood shavings are laid out for a soft place to walk around in his stall.

Now it's time for his warmup. Crackerjack is lunged by his trainer. This means he works his gaits in a circle in both right and left directions with a long rope. He walks, trots, canters, stops and starts on command. This helps him turn his brain on and listen to the trainer who is in charge.

Therapy sessions are next. The therapist plans how hippotherapy will be used to help address a rider's needs while working with the horse handler. Breaks in between sessions are taken, with snacks, hay and water. Treats are given when he works hard. Treats include: apples, carrots, and peppermint candies.

Dinner time! Grains, hay and water are what is served in a bucket and feeding/watering trough. A quick brush down to wipe the sweat follows. Now it's time to go outdoors and run in the pasture for the evening.

Therapy horses work with individualized work schedules and training/conditioning programs. Special care is taken to ensure their health and emotional well-being. Crackerjack and the therapists who work with him help those with many different special needs.

Some people come in walking while others may have a wheelchair or a walker. Hippotherapy is good for people who are young or old, girl or boy, mute (doesn't talk) or never ending talking. New riders and experienced riders are all welcome. Horses are inclusive to all and Crackerjack accepts everyone!

Meet the Contributors

Akyra Kikumoto is daughter #2, and the first to have Apraxia of Speech. When her therapist mentioned including hippotherapy, and because her mom was raised on a horse ranch, it was a perfect match! Akyra rode Whinny, and miniature horse Toby is referenced in the stall next to Crackerjack in the barn. Akyra never crawled, even with mom trying daily to teach her. She is now a successful pre-teen planning her design future on HGTV. She enjoys connecting with friends and playing golf with her dad.

Amaya Kikumoto is daughter #3, and also has CAS. Amaya didn't speak until age 4, and at age 6 was crowned IJM Colorado Jr Princess and competed on an international stage in Nashville. She proudly gave a 45 second tear-jerking speech! All due to the power of the horse's movement! Amaya was extremely afraid of her horse Crackerjack, and it took over a month to even get on him. But when she did, magic happened and her confidence skyrocketed! Amaya currently enjoys competitive dance, Miss National Showbiz Petite, golf and basketball.

Akayla Kikumoto is
daughter #4, and the second
to last to have CAS in the
family. Akayla is a spitfire and
as an Irish twin to Amaya,
she was not going to let her
sister out do her in anything!
Her favorite horse to ride at
therapy was Crackerjack,
who she nicknamed CJ, after
her only brother, who also
has CAS. Akayla currently loves
competitive dance, and competed
in her first hip hop solo to a song,
Bubblegum Wiggle. She has won
several accolades in dance.
She loves playing golf and basketball .

Meet the Author

AJ Kikumoto is an up and coming female author and owner of Yellow Daisy Publishing Company. She is a super mom to 6 kids, 4 of whom have the invisible disability of Childhood Apraxia of Speech (CAS). Her Master's degree in Elementary Education has come in handy while taking on the challenges of guiding her kids through the difficulties of Apraxia of Speech. The many hours of therapy, and different challenges with each kid, proved an ever-changing learning atmosphere and mode of communication. She was fed up by the lack of awareness and lack of education in CAS. She authored this book based on her own personal experiences. She encourages moms to rely on their "mommy gut." Mother knows best!!

AJ uses her expertise from dancing with the NBA Denver Nuggets Dancers and currently coaches a youth dance team, empowering the girls to follow their dreams, believe in themselves, and be 21st century boss babes in these unprecedented times. As a competitor for Mrs. Colorado America, her legacy project is promoting #beautyisinclusion and #youcandohardthings. This is based on true events in the "Zoey's Great Adventures" book series. She teaches parents and children alike, the power of a positive mindset, anti-bullying, and promoting good morals and values in our society. A portion of the proceeds will be donated to the nonprofit Apraxia Kids at Apraxia-Kids.org. She believes in paying forward.